For my Dad

Whales

MAGIC *of the* OCEAN

Warner Treasures is a trademark of
Warner Books, Inc.

Warner Books, Inc.,
1271 Avenue of the Americas,
New York, NY 10020

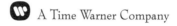 A Time Warner Company

Printed in Mexico
First Printing: March 1995
10 9 8 7 6 5 4 3 2 1

ISBN: 0-446-91011-2

Whales

by Barbara Jane Zitwer

MAGIC of the OCEAN

Illustrations by Robbin Gourley

WARNER ⚙ TREASURES ™
PUBLISHED BY WARNER BOOKS
A TIME WARNER COMPANY

They say the sea is cold
but the sea contains the hottest blood of all.
— D. H. Lawrence, "Whales Weep Not"

THE MAGIC OF WHALES HAS BEEN known to humans since they first discovered these enormous creatures of the sea. From the time people first heard the haunting and beautiful songs of the whales, we have been fascinated by these enchanting beings. Throughout literature, art, movies, and music, there have been many myths about, and magical powers attributed to, whales.

Today, because of the attention and study directed to our mammal relations, we are beginning to find out about the intelligence, power, and gentleness of the majestic whales. As we unlock their great mystery, we may also gain a better understanding of ourselves.

BABY ANNOUNCEMENT:

CONGRATULATIONS, IT'S A BOUNCING baby boy! A humpback . . . and what a boy he is . . . he's twenty-five feet long and weighs two tons!

Whales give birth to only one calf every two or three years. The gestation period differs between 10¾ months and 1¼ years, depending on the species of whale. Mother whales

always nurse their calves and produce up to two hundred pounds of milk daily. The calves gain two hundred pounds a day!

The calf will nurse for seven months to a year, and it stays very close to Mom, often resting on her back for comfort, for over a year, and it will never leave her side, unless she is killed.

Calves are born in the warm tropical waters and are the last to travel north in the winter. Not only mothers, but the entire pack of whales protect the young.

It was once reported that off the coast of Spain, a small calf was harpooned and the mother whale stayed with her child, tugging the harpoon lines until she freed the baby. Using her flippers, she cradled it and swam with it to freedom far out in the ocean away from danger and humans.

DIETING

A WHALE FOODFEST CAN LAST TWENTY-four hours a day for days at a time. They can consume over two tons of food each day! An average blue whale eats constantly for four months and then fasts for the remaining eight months.

A blue whale's stomach is eighty-seven feet long and can contain five million shrimp when filled. Most whales can swallow food no larger than the size of a grapefruit. They exist eating minuscule plankton, shrimp, fishes, and other tiny animals and plants of the sea in huge amounts. Blue whales have no teeth.

IF YOU GET THEM ALL RIGHT, CONGRATU-lations to you! Flip to page 38 and make yourself a "Blue Whale."

1. What actress had her leg bitten off by a killer whale and in what movie?

2. Who played Captain Ahab in MOBY DICK?

3. Who starred in LITTLE NEMO? (Lumiere Bros. film, 1909)

4. What actress plays the marine biologist and heroine of STAR TREK IV: THE VOYAGE HOME and what kind of whales does the *Enterprise* save?

Answers:
1) Bo Derek in *Orca*
2) Gregory Peck
3) John Bunny
4) Catherine Hicks; humpback whales

WHALE ROMANCE

IT IS NO WONDER THAT WHEN A MALE whale finds a mate he wants, he usually gets her. He sings songs of love, haunting, melodic tunes heard underneath the tropical waters where he croons to his beloved.

Females can be very choosy and difficult; they swim to shallow waters and turn belly-up if they don't want to be made love to, because mating occurs belly-to-belly.

It is not certain, but females and males seem to return often to exactly the same spots to mate and give birth to their young. This might indicate that whales could be monogamous, or at least according to species and specific grouping.

WHALE BODY LANGUAGE

Breaching:

BREACHING IS AN UNPREDICTABLE movement in which a whale completely jumps out of the sea in a horizontal movement. The whale virtually ejects its humongous body from the ocean. Can you imagine 100,000 pounds of whale jettisoned into the sky in front of your eyes? This action can take place in a moment, and then the whale will disappear as if it had never been there.

Whales

Whales breach for several reasons: they may be surprised by a predator or fishing boat, or alarmed for some other reason. Breaching is an immense movement that can warn or scare off any potential threat.

Breaching is also a form of just plain fun! It's an exuberant display of excitement for a whale.

Breaching is sometimes interpreted as a form of communication between whales — you can imagine the sound a whale makes as it slaps back down on the ocean — it's like a forty-ton tree trunk falling on the ground, and the sound waves can be heard by other whales for miles. Whales also breach when they enter a group of others — it's a form of saying, "I'm here!" or they breach to get rid of an unruly member of the group.

Babies are found to breach more often than elders. They're frisky, they want to have fun, and it's also a way to slowly separate from their moms.

It is also believed that breaching is performed to cleanse the whales' bodies of barnacles and other sea debris that builds up on their thick skin.

SPYLOPPING

WHALES ARE NATURALLY INTERESTED in what is going on around them, both in and out of the water. Sometimes they will just pop their kidney-shaped eyes out of the ocean at eye level to have a look around — this action is known as spylopping. Their eyes are situated on opposite sides of their heads and can appear either funny or weird looking, depending on how you view things.

A whale's eyes are truly fish-eyed, like a camera lens. They are created in this way so that they can see in the refractive ocean waters as well as having good vision in the air by rolling their eyes back to the flattened portion of their eye lens. This circular eye lens is well suited for both water and air, and whales' eyes are also equipped with a coating of shock-absorbing tissues so they are protected when they immerse in the sea.

It is not really understood yet why whales peer out of the sea; it might be that they are just curious. . .only time and more investigation will reveal their true motives.

17

TAILSLAPPING

WHALES' TAILS DIFFER from those of fish in their construction. As opposed to fish, whose tails move sideways, whales' tails move up and down. The tail of the humpback whale is a third the size of its entire body, and is used to navigate, to manipulate prey, and to make sounds.

There are reasons for these, as there are for all whale movements. When a whale slaps its tail in a rapid movement, it expends a tremendous amount of energy. It might be to caution an oncoming vessel, to signal to its fellow group members that a predator is near, or as an actual weapon in its defense against a

killer whale or white shark. The barnacle-encrusted tail is a powerful weapon and is razor-sharp.

When a whale experiences agitation or anxiety, it may tailslap, or when in a good and relaxed mood, it might flip its tail as if it were a happy puppy.

Slow, sensual tailslapping is also a form of male courtship and can really turn on a female whale — the moves, the style, the sounds, and the size of a male's tail can make the difference between a couple's mating or not.

One of the only ways in which whales can show their emotions is through the movements of their tails and of their entire bodies. These might not at first sound like delicate movements, but in the context of the size of the ocean and the anatomy of such huge animals, they are graceful, and one can view whales as dancers of the sea. Each movement is deliberate and means something. As the crook of a head, the twirl of a pretty girl's shoulder-length hair, or the stance of a handsome man can turn on a human of the opposite sex, so can each movement of the whale for a prospective mate.

RULES FOR WHALE WATCHERS

1. Never whale-watch in a rowboat or kayak; although most whales are gentle creatures, they can be unpredictable, and a flap of their tails can capsize a small vessel.

2. Bring a copy of a nice long book to read — why not *Moby Dick*? It might take hours before you spot a whale, and meanwhile you can enjoy a whale of a tale. Whales are unpredictable and can appear and disappear in the flutter of an eyelid.

3. Bring binoculars along. . .whales might swim far off in the distance, and you wouldn't want to miss a sighting, especially after sailing in ocean waters for hours.

4. If the whales come up close to you in the boat, don't inhale the vapor from their blowholes — the vapor can contain dangerous bacteria and viruses.

5. Don't aim your camera too close to the

spray from the whales' blowholes; the spray contains oils that can damage a camera lens.

6. On a sunny day, watch for rainbows that the whales create when blowing spray from their blowholes. The sunlight reflects off the water droplets, creating a dazzling display of color.

7. Keep the motor running at all times while you are in your boat, because that will alert a

whale that a visitor is nearby. If they know you're about, they won't hurt you.

8. Don't ever, ever surprise a whale— they don't like it and you won't like how they may react!

AMBERGRIS — TO DOUSE AND AROUSE

AMBERGRIS IS A waxy substance, secreted by some whales, that is used in making perfume. In Chinese, ambergris was called Lung Yen, or Devil's Saliva. It was considered a powerful aphrodisiac and was more valuable than gold, with its worth gaining century by century.

Oddly, ambergris, which is such a

romantic and sensual product for humans, is actually created inside the bowels of a sperm whale. It is formed around indigestible squid beaks that get stuck in a whale's intestines. For the whale, the beginning of ambergris can lead to heartburn, stomach problems, constipation, and sometimes death due to a total blockage of the bowels. Ambergris is the greasy oil that forms to help eradicate the irritation from the beaks, but it is deadly to the whale and can grow and grow into hundreds of pounds of substance stuck in the poor animal's belly.

Ambergris was mentioned in the writings of Marco Polo, and during the Renaissance, its price soared because it became a valuable ingredient in the making of perfume.

A whaling company found the largest piece of ambergris ever in 1912. It weighed in at over 1,000 pounds and was sold for over $60,000. Today the price fluctuates between $100 and $150 per pound and with sperm whale fishing

becoming outlawed in most every part of the world, the price and value of natural ambergris just goes up.

While ambergris can kill an eighty-ton whale, it can also seduce the most beautiful woman in the world — or so it's said.

SECRETS OF LONGEVITY

THE OIL FOUND IN WHALES WAS NOT ONLY used to light lamps and for all sorts of industrial purposes in the making of products, but it also had a medicinal use. The nature of the oil is such that it makes an excellent preservative.

It was believed that the oil from a whale could cure certain ailments such as rheumatism and arthritis. When a whale was found beached on an island shore, natives with severe physical problems would be brought to the dead animal. There is a story of an old man from Petite Nevis in Bequia who was brought to a beached sperm whale. The

poor man was crippled and twisted in arthritic pain. A sling was made, and his entire body was dipped into the huge deposit of oil in the whale's head. He lay in the oil for a long time, and when he was lifted out, he felt much better. He reported later on that his condition was greatly improved. This occurred in 1969, not hundreds of years ago. Other medicinal uses for whale oil:

1. relieves headaches
2. soothes strains & sprains
3. prevents colds
4. acts as a powerful laxative
5. elixir to prolong life

SCRIMSHAW AND STOMACHERS

SCRIMSHAW IS A PURELY AMERICAN folk art that began at the height of whaling in America. Whalers were considered the lowest of the low, much as artists are regarded in society today, until they're "discovered." It was perhaps through their art and the creations of scrimshaw, that whalers found dignity, pride, and a special sense of themselves.

The first appearance of scrimshaw was in the log of a whaling boat, *By Chance* (1825–1826). Fishermen practiced this art during lulls in fishing and when they had free time. The word *scrimshaw* comes from *scrim,* meaning "to trace," and *shaw,* meaning "bone."

There were always extra whale bones, teeth, and other materials lying on deck, and they were given to the whalers. The men carved with anything they could find: jackknives, files, needles, or hacksaws. After they carved the image, they used various inks to dye the etched image so that it would stand out brightly from the ivory color of the bone.

Walking sticks were popular, as were necklaces and jewelry, but one of the most popular forms of scrimshaw was used for women's corsets. This object became known as the "stomacher" and was

Whales

a flattened piece of bone, usually carved for the
sailor's loved one. It was a plate inserted into a
corset to flatten a woman's stomach. These were
made with great care by sailors, and sometimes
poems were etched into the stomachers such as
the following:

> This bone once in a sperm's whale jaw did rest
> Now 'tis intended for a woman's breast.
> This my love I do intend
> For thee to use and not to lend.

Accept dear girl this busk from me
Carved by my humble hand
I took it from a sperm whale's jaw
One thousand miles from land.

In many a gale has been the whale,
In which this bone did nest
His time is past, his bone at last
Must now support thy breast.

— From *Folklore and the Sea*,
   © The Maritime Historical Association,
      Inc. 1973 by Horace Palmer Beck

In all the works of scrimshaw, there is a proficiency of craftsmanship and detailed designs. The art form still exists today, and most common scrimshaw is used for pocketbooks and lamps. Because of laws protecting whales,

synthetic materials are used, and synthetic reproductions of original scrimshaw designs are now popular in gift shops throughout New England.

WHALE MYTHS AND LORE

ESKIMOS FROM ALASKA AND Siberia performed lengthy ceremonies before going out to hunt for their prey. Such preparations were important to these people, because the food and oil from the whales were essential to their survival. Men, women, and children joined in for days of dancing, eating, singing, and praying.

Native Americans who believed whales to be so powerful that the sight of them would scare off their enemies carved huge totems with whale figures to upset their foes.

Arabian myth told of whales that were the supporters of the world.

In the Moslem religion, a whale is one of the ten creatures in heaven.

The ancient Japanese believed that whales were an omen of war. The whale's mouth was thought to be a gateway to another world.

THE MEN WHO HUNTED WHALES

AMONG ALL THE SAILORS, WHALERS HAD the lowest status. Although they bravely risked their lives hunting the most feared creatures of the sea, their wages were less than those of any other sailor; their boats the filthiest. They were scorned and mocked. Other fishermen could pick out a whaler a mile away by his hunched-over, depressed look and his tattered garments.

Today, if a whaler spoke to his therapist, he would unload his anxieties and fears about harpooning these enormous creatures, how day after day his life was at risk. He would lie on the couch and recall in horror how a sperm whale was lifted

onto the deck, its belly sliced open, two tons of krill, shrimp, fish, and blood pouring out and filling the sailors' nostrils with a stench so great it was hard not to faint. It was a horrible, horrible job.

Villagers ran when a whaler approached the harbor. It was reported once that a whaling ship landed off the coast of New England, and the smell from the decks was so putrid that it pervaded the entire village. The captain was ordered to go back to the ocean immediately and clean his ship before he was allowed to land and his men to stand firm on the ground again.

RECIPE FOR A "BLUE WHALE"

1 oz. vodka

1 oz. blue curaçao

2 oz. rum

Pour into blender filled with crushed ice. Add a teaspoon of sea salt, for that refreshing flavor.

WHITE WHALES AND UNICORNS OF THE SEA

WHITE WHALES ONLY LIVE WHERE IT IS white — in the frigid and icy waters of the Arctic. They play and feed, and mate and live in a winter wonderland, and they blend in with icebergs and their environment.

There are two types of whales that are white: the beluga whale and its cousin the narwhal. Both belugas and narwhals also have teeth, as opposed to other species such as humpbacks.

Belugas get their name from the Russian word for "white," and there are true white specimens, but most often they are mottled in color. Belugas are very cute looking and have rounded heads with smiling mouths. They are easy to imagine as cuddly stuffed animals. Belugas, among the smallest whales, live a short time; twenty years is an average life span.

Their cousins the narwhals are known as "unicorns of the sea," for they have a unique

Whales

horn-like tusk that protrudes from their heads.
These horns only grow on male whales. In ancient
times, their horns were sought after as greedily as
ambergris and were thought to possess magical
powers. Men would grind the ivory horn into a
fine powder and mix it into mysterious potions to
drink, thinking its consumption would bring them

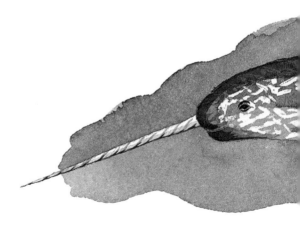

health and sexual prowess. So rare and precious were the horns of these creatures that it is recorded in ancient books that during the Middle Ages, an Elector of Saxony paid a week's wages for one tusk and also that the Prussian Kaiser Karl V paid off a national debt with two horns!

Whales

KILLER WHALES, WITH THEIR DISTINCTIVE black and white markings and sharp, fierce-looking teeth, are perhaps the smartest of all animals and the most feared among the warm-blooded

creatures of the sea. They are savage and will attack their own, seals, dolphins, other whale species, and others.

However, killer whales have a fondness for humans. They have such a keen intelligence and learning ability that they have become the stars of many aquatic shows. In captivity, killers are friendly and charming. They have never been known to attack or harm people.

THE SONGS OF WHALES

THE EARLIEST REFERENCE TO SONGS OF the ocean can be found in Homer's epic *The Odyssey,* where it is described that sirens sang and lured fishermen to their doom. Songs from the ocean were only a myth until 1952, when a marine scientist first heard the songs of whales and identified them as such. His name was Frank Watlington and he and his wife were the first humans to study and record the songs of whales.

Each song is composed of short sounds, or "notes," and each song has a different and distinct theme. A song may last from six to twenty minutes. Songs are sung by adult humpback whales. All whales in a specific region sing the same songs, and the songs change season to season. Each

season a song

changes slightly, so after several years, the songs will evolve into a new theme. Whales imitate each other and learn from each other.

While singing they are motionless with their heads facing downward into the sea, flippers stretched out and tail upward toward the surface. They appear very relaxed while singing, and perhaps that is why their songs are beautiful, soulful melodies that can relax a human listener and even put you to sleep. Whale songs have been used as backgrounds by Judy Collins and Paul Winter, and the album *Songs of the Humpback Whale* has sold more than 100,000 copies. It has been selling for years.

A WHALE OF A STORY...OR A POEM

And I was full of dreams.
Dreams, dreams, dreams. And I dream still.
And the whale is a dream.
— Hubert Selby, "Of Whales and Dreams"

Whales

THE MOST POPULAR STORY OF WHALES is probably the biblical fable of Jonah and the Whale. Many versions of that story have been told throughout the centuries. But whales are not just the subject of moral fables. They evoke dreams and beauty, tranquility and majesty.

The avant-garde composer John Cage wrote a musical piece called *Litany for a Whale,* and Leonard Bernstein wrote *The Moby Diptych.*

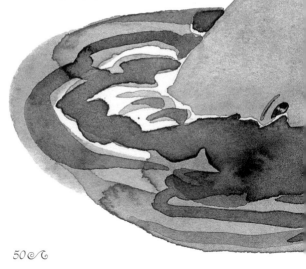

Rudyard Kipling, in his wonderful *Just So Stories,* wrote the glorious tale "How the Whale Got His Throat," which uses the myth of Jonah and the Whale as a basis.

Carlo Collodi took his puppet Pinocchio into the bowels of a whale in *The Adventures of Pinocchio.*

Other writers who have immortalized whales in many different ways are:

Margaret Atwood, "The Afterlife of Ishmael"

David Mamet, *The Whale*

David Rabe, *First Whale*

James Dickey, "In Lace and Whale Bone"

Derek Wolcott, "The Whale, His Bulwark"

W. S. Merwin, "Leviathan"

Allen Ginsberg, "Have You Seen the Movie"

Whales

Rabelais, *Gargantua and Pantagruel*

Rudolph E. Raspe, *Baron Munchausen*

Unknown Swahili writer, "King Suleimani and the Whale"

Unknown writer of famous Jewish fable, "An Old Man, His Son, and a Fish"

Jun Honda, Japanese poet, "Walk Inside a Whale"

Robert Lowell, "The Quaker Graveyard in Nantucket"

Other whale reading can be found in works by Pablo Neruda, Lawrence Ferlinghetti, D. M. Thomas, John Fowles, Peter Sis, and many others. Both in children's literature and adult fiction, whether it be modern or hundreds of years old, the subject of whales reappears often.

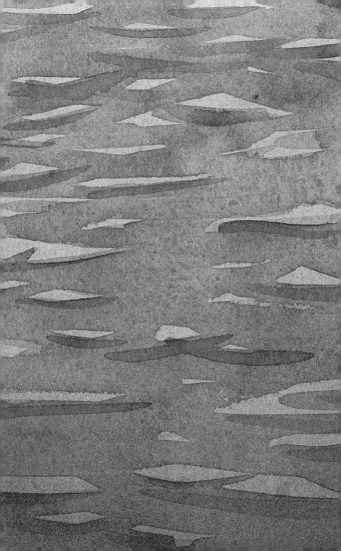